Norman St John-Stevas M

BETTER SCHOOLS FOR ALL

A Conservative approach to
the problems of the
comprehensive school

CPC NO. 617

ISBN 0 85070 611 4

Published by the Conservative Political Centre,
32 Smith Square, London SW1P 3HH and printed by
Strange the Printer Limited, Eastbourne
First published 1977

Contents

Acknowledgements

THIS STUDY OF COMPREHENSIVE SCHOOLS is the latest instalment of the educational policy review which was set in train by the Conservative Party two years ago and which has led to the formulation of a number of proposals on standards, parental rights, the assisted places scheme, etc. I am grateful to all those who have let me have their views and who have done research work over this period. This pamphlet is really the tip of an iceberg which represents many months of work by those in the Tory Party with a particular interest in education. I would like to thank especially Mr Paul Williams, of *The Sunday Telegraph*, who has coped with and sifted the material and has helped me continually with the preparation of the booklet.

Amongst those to whom I would like to express my thanks are Mr Stuart Sexton, Mr John Houston, Miss Biddy Passmore and Mr John Ranelagh of the Conservative Research Department. I am grateful also for a number of valuable suggestions made by Miss Janet Fookes MP and her study group on standards in our schools. The Conservative Political Centre carried out a survey through its discussion groups in the constituencies during 1976. The 551 reports received have been most helpful in ascertaining the views of 'the grass roots'. I am also happy to acknowledge the assistance given by the National Advisory Committee on Education and the Young Conservatives.

'We must beware of trying to build a society in which nobody counts for anything except a politician or an official, a society where enterprise gains no reward and thrift no privileges. Human beings are endowed with infinitely varying qualities and dispositions and each one is different from the other. We cannot make them all the same. It would be a pretty dull world if we did. It is in our power, however, to secure equal opportunities for all.'

(*Winston Churchill, Broadcast speech*, 21st March 1943)

1. Background and history

THE DEBATE over comprehensive schools shows no signs of abating.

More than most political and education arguments, it has become clouded by misconceptions, over-simplifications, mis-representations and exaggerations. Thus a mythology has been built up that, while Labour supporters care only for comprehensive schooling and are indifferent to standards, Conservatives are concerned principally with the maintenance of grammar schools and little with the educationally disadvantaged or equality of educational opportunity. These stereotypes, seductive though they may be, bear little relation to reality. I hope that this short study will help to dispel them.

Most parents, whatever their political persuasion, care little for the way in which schools are organised but are desperately concerned about standards. Their doubts about comprehensive schools, and their desire to preserve established grammar schools of proven worth, are by-products of their interest in high standards of educational attainment. This concern constitutes the common ground on which, given goodwill and good sense, it should be possible to build a sensible national education policy.

Over the past three years the major theme of Conservative education policy has been the preservation and promotion of quality and the raising of educational standards, and in advancing this cause we have been able to draw upon a Tory tradition which goes back for at least a century. We have set our faces against what Matthew Arnold singled out as the aim of socialist educational theorists, 'the elimination of superiorities'. Conservatives want to encourage every child to develop to the full the unique gifts which he or she enjoys. We want to encourage and not to hold back the able child for both individual and national reasons. If Britain is to hold an honoured place in the modern world, quality must become the hallmark of the nation in this century, as it was in the last, and the place to start a revolution in favour of pride in work and high standards is in the schools.

We reject the socialist obsession with equality which threatens to destroy all that is best in our educational system. Conservatives see the school not as an instrument for dubious social engineering but as a vehicle for promoting quality and educational values. What is needed is a flexible system with a varied curriculum which will cater for children of different capacities and gifts. The 'less able' academically may well be the 'more able' in other respects. We see the most effective way of achieving our aims not through a monolithic system in which there is only one type of school for every type of child but through one in which a variety of schools can flourish and co-exist.

Our educational system is now principally a comprehensive one and is likely to remain so in the future; but within this comprehensive framework there is room for a certain number of specialised and selective schools. It would be socially divisive and a major abridgement of educational opportunity if the only selective schools were to be found in the private sector and confined to those children with parents affluent enough to pay the fees. The Conservative assisted places scheme, which would help parents of modest means to send their children to good selective schools, is designed to extend parental choice – not absolutely, for this is impossible in practice – but to the greatest possible extent.

Conservatives in education are looking forward, not back. While we would never have undermined the independence of local education authorities by dictating from the centre that they should re-organise their schools on comprehensive lines, we recognise that as a result of this policy the great majority of our children are now being educated in comprehensive schools. Out of the total secondary school population[1] in maintained

[1] See DES press notice of 12th August 1977. According to the statistics in this release, 3,076 secondary schools, including sixth form colleges, were comprehensive in January 1977. A further 564 were middle schools, deemed secondary, which form part of a comprehensive system. There

schools of 4,039,000 in January 1977, 3,221,000 (79·7 per cent) were in comprehensive or middle (deemed secondary) schools. That is why I stated at the Party Conference at Blackpool in October 1977 that 'we must devote the major part of our effort to improving the comprehensive schools'. Our aim must be to reform and mould the system of comprehensive schools in a way that will reproduce the best of the grammar school tradition in this new setting.

Conservative education policies are moderate, sensible and practical, as this booklet shows, and I hope that we may be able in time to re-establish a consensus so that education will be taken out of party politics. The future of our children is far too important to jeopardise it by treating them as party political footballs. Yet it would be too high a price to pay for this desirable end to follow in education a policy of unconditional surrender to the follies and false conclusions of political dogma in education. Children have been the victims of the attempts to impose comprehensive schools everywhere, regardless of parental wishes, local conditions and financial resources. We must now come to their aid and put those things right which have gone wrong. The comprehensive ideal has been brought into disrepute by the excesses of socialist theorists and education ministers. The Labour Party may fairly be said to have behaved as the enemy of the comprehensive school; and, *mutatis mutandis*, the Tory Party with its practical and reforming approach to education is its best friend.

There are signs that in some respects the political parties are moving closer together on educational matters. I welcome the conversion of Mr Callaghan and Mrs Williams to much of what the Conservative Party has been saying on standards and parental rights and influence. That is all to the good. Mrs Williams, if a free agent, would clearly return to an older Labour tradition which lays stress, not on impossible equalities, but on high standards, academic excellence, and the importance of providing a ladder of opportunity for the bright child from a disavdantaged home.

were 842 secondary modern schools, 407 grammar and 99 technical and other types of secondary school making a total number of schools of 4,988.

Unfortunately she is not acting on her own and the party pressures to which she is subject have already stultified some of her important initiatives on providing for the clever child in comprehensive schools, reforming the curriculum and improving the quality of teaching. Nevertheless she may be able to bring about necessary reforms in education, and she can rely on the support of the Opposition in so doing. I hope she will be successful, but my hopes are greater than my expectations. We shall see.

Secondary education since 1944

Secondary education as we know it began with the 1944 Education Act. Before that time, most children stayed on to the age of 14 in all-age schools. Some were able to go on to secondary education, but only 25 per cent of the places at secondary schools were free. The others had to be paid for.

The 1944 Act, which was the brainchild of R. A. (now Lord) Butler, established free secondary education for all up to the school-leaving age, which was increased from 14 to 15 in 1947. It also allowed for a further increase up to 16. This was implemented much later, under Mrs Thatcher in 1972. The Act required local authorities to see that primary and secondary schools were available for all. But it did **not** lay down what kind of schools they should be, any more than it insisted that they should be provided by local authorities.

The tri-partite system of grammar, secondary and technical schools was a recommendation of the White Paper which preceded the Act and was based on the work of three inquiries into secondary education in 1926 (Hadow), 1938 (Spens) and 1943 (Norwood). It seemed then to be an effective way of setting up a secondary education system for all. Three types of school were to be provided so that each child could receive the education to which he was best suited. The ideal was 'parity of esteem' for the schools, so that to go to a secondary modern school would not be considered better or worse than going to a grammar school.

The difficulties of selection were appreciated, and it was

emphasised that there should be a maximum of flexibility and ease of transfer from one type of school to another. Local authorities were urged to treat the schools on an equal basis when it came to the provision of accommodation and amenities. But this ideal was not achieved generally. Few technical schools were set up. In reality, the three types of school did not achieve that parity of esteem. In most cases they were not considered equal by parents or pupils, or even by teachers and local authorities. Standards of provision were not the same. The 11-plus became a stigma of failure.

Where true equality between the schools was not achieved, it was not a fault of the principle or of the system. The fault lay in the way the system was implemented. This is amply demonstrated by those cases where equality was achieved, where the so-called second-class secondary modern schools were admirable and popular institutions, often developing their own sixth forms.

With the growth of the attitude that secondary modern education was in some way inferior, opposition grew to the whole concept of selection – as did the belief that the answer was a system where each secondary school catered for all abilities. Grammar, technical and secondary education would all be provided within one set of walls. This in essence is the comprehensive school.

As debate began in the 1950s, it was relatively non-partisan. The decision facing those who were concerned was whether to make the extra effort to improve the existing system, or to put that effort into evolving the new system of comprehensive education.

This was a decision for the local communities, as represented by their local councils. The role of the government of the day was to act as a long stop, to intervene only where it appeared to it that a council was going badly wrong.

And so it was that as early as the late 1940s and throughout the 1950s the first steps towards comprehensive education were taken. Anglesey was the first. London started building purpose-built comprehensive schools. Coventry and Leicestershire reorganised. A system of education based on different ages of transfer, with middle schools, was pioneered in the West Riding and

Bradford. More and more authorities decided that comprehensive education was worth investigating and implementing.

The councils that took these decisions were of all political complexions. The government in power, which was Conservative from 1951 onwards, had no objections: it was considered healthy to see the wide variety of local initiatives being taken. Conservatives were not against comprehensive education. Education was, and is, an evolving discipline, and changes are necessary for evolution. It would take some years of seeing the different systems in action before lessons could be drawn as to the advantages and success of each one.

But in the early 1960s there came a development which was to cause lasting harm to Britain's schools. In the Labour Party, comprehensive education ceased to be the subject of discussion, and became instead the object of political dogma. Commonsense, practicalities, realities, suffered as a consequence.

In 1965 the Labour government issued its notorious circular 10/65. This called on local authorities to change to comprehensive education. It was the first step towards the removal of the freedom of local authorities to develop their own educational systems. Although the circular professed that the Government did not seek to impose destructive or over-rapid change, the Government in effect resorted to financial blackmail to get its own way. In Circular 10/66 (March 1966), Mr Crosland threatened to withhold approval for new secondary school building projects unless they could be fitted into a comprehensive pattern. The actual needs of the children were ignored. The deliberate use by the Government of money as a political weapon had consequences from which a whole generation of children suffered, through overcrowded classrooms.

Faced with the alternative of being denied permission to borrow money to finance new school buildings, most authorities capitulated and produced comprehensive schemes. These schemes were not put forward because they were best for children, but to satisfy Labour's political demands. Eventually the Labour government decided to drop its blackmail tactics, and opt for straightforward compulsion through a Parliamentary Act. But it was defeated in the 1970 General Election before the Act could be passed.

The new Conservative government of 1970 immediately withdrew Circular 10/65. It also rejected Labour's example of imposing systems of education; those authorities that wished to pursue comprehensive systems, and whose schemes were acceptable, were allowed to continue with them. Local authorities that did so included those that were Labour and Conservative controlled.

When the Labour government resumed power in 1974, it also resumed its ambition of removing from local authorities their freedom to organise education as they saw fit, and forcing them to go comprehensive. My colleagues and I spent many hours of argument trying to improve what was to become the Education Act 1976. Accepting that the Labour-controlled House of Commons wanted such a Bill, we tried to make it a good Bill by including elements of commonsense. Time after time our suggestions were rejected out of an irrational fear that we were trying to kill the Bill. For example, we wanted to allow local authorities some freedom to develop schools with specialities, but the only selection allowed by the Government was for music. Specialisation in mathematics, languages, sport or anything else was ruled out.

The future

Even a number of Labour supporters are now worried that the headlong dash to comprehensive schools regardless of consequences is causing harm. The Government is showing a much healthier concern for education than it has for a long time. Yet even that concern has not been allowed to temper the enthusiasm for forcing authorities to go comprehensive.

Conservatives will repeal the 1976 Education Act when we return to power. We believe it is wrong for the Government to dictate the type of organisation local authorities should adopt in education. And it follows from this that we will not seek to force local authorities to adopt any other form of organisation.

There is no question of our seeking a return to the tri-partite system. Although we are likely to return to power before many authorities have completed their reorganisation, it is probable that some will wish to continue along that path even when compulsion is removed. We would not wish to hinder them, providing they have planned to avoid the problems that are now becoming obvious.

The problem that faces the next Conservative government, then, is not how to unscramble comprehensive reorganisation already carried out. It is how to ensure that comprehensive schools really do work for the bright, average and below average child. It is how to undo the harm done by the Labour Party's disregard for classroom realities.

Comprehensive schools are here to stay. We must take the new organisation, improve it where necessary, but above all we must make it work. What the problems are, and the methods of tackling them, are the subject of the rest of this booklet.

2. The problems

GRAVE PROBLEMS face many of the country's secondary schools. They are not of the teachers' making. They have been caused by the indecent haste of reorganisation, forced on local authorities by Labour governments and, in some cases, endorsed by Labour-controlled councils. The result has been the creation by the socialists of a crisis of confidence in the very subject of their dogmatic diligence, the comprehensive school.

These problems are not inherent in the comprehensive idea. They have been caused by the failure to allow schools to evolve in their own time. The energy and resources that should have gone into improving all schools have been diverted to reorganisation. The attempt to achieve the highest possible standards for all children has been set back at least ten years as a result. Where secondary modern schools still exist, it is just as important to raise their standards as it is to raise the standards of poor comprehensive schools that often started life as poor secondary moderns. In so many cases changing the name and the system has done nothing to change the difficulties that always existed.

In discussing solutions to the problems, then, we should not consider a typical school, but a typical problem school. Teachers and parents know that too many of them do exist. Our approach should above all be practical.

Consider a large comprehensive school, say 1,800 pupils, in a poor urban area with mainly council housing. The school is an amalgamation of two poor secondary modern schools, and is on at least two sites separated by a mile. The intake of the school is entirely from that poor urban area, where there are considerable racial problems. The head is a weak man, who allows teachers to work as they see fit. Some have set up mixed-ability classes, more for ideological than educational reasons.

The only remedial teacher is a part-timer. Because the head

believes strongly in sport, he has distributed senior posts more on sporting ability than responsibility in the classroom. There are no special classes for intelligent children because he does not believe there are any in the school. There are major problems of vandalism and indiscipline, but the head does not use the cane. He blames the primary schools for failing in their task.

Because the school is unpopular, it has a large proportion of poor teachers who could not get jobs elsewhere in the days when there was a teacher shortage, and the school could not attract good teachers.

These are not exaggerated or fanciful problems. It would be an unfortunate school that had them all at once, but in any discussion on reforms it is as well to look at this scenario and ask: will this reform or that one help such a school?

Internal and external problems

There are two sorts of problems facing comprehensive schools: external problems, caused by lack of resources, the form of reorganisation adopted by a local authority and the school's environment; and internal problems, caused by the wide range of ability and the heavy demands made by society on the curriculum.

The final stage of Labour's reorganisation programme has come at a time when resources have never been scarcer. But even in the mid-sixties, reorganisation was carried out without sufficient assistance from the Government, creating a heavy burden on local communities. Many schemes are disfigured by oversized schools, split sites, inadequate facilities and temporary accommodation. And very little attention has been paid to solving the most intransigent difficulty, the neighbourhood school.

Inside the school, the attempt to cater for all abilities has led to over-diversification of the curriculum, with inefficient use of staff and plant as a result. The comprehensive ideal has been accompanied by the concept of mixed-ability teaching and new teaching methods, both of which have given rise to concern. There is also the difficult question of when to specialise.

Another alarming development is the decline of moral and religious education in comprehensive schools. The Education Act of 1944 lays down clearly and unequivocally that there is a duty to provide religious instruction in all schools and that each day should begin with a collective act of worship attended by all pupils. The varying backgrounds and beliefs of pupils at comprehensive schools present a great challenge to teachers of religious education, while the sheer size of the schools and – particularly in split-site schools – the absence of a hall large enough to accommodate all the pupils, make collective worship difficult. These problems must be faced with determination. I believe that I am speaking for the majority of parents in the country when I say that we want to see religious education continue in our schools and that children should have the opportunity of praying together.

Need for an inquiry

The war of statistics waged by both sides of the debate is not helping to resolve the argument about educational standards and comprehensive schools. Some studies lead one to believe that standards may be falling. On the other hand some of the early studies produced by the defenders of comprehensive schools are statistically dubious to say the least.[1] Recently they have pointed to the increasing number of exam passes. But there have also been suggestions that the standards needed for exam passes have fallen, and that examiners pass a fixed percentage of entries rather than mark by fixed criteria.

These arguments can be resolved to everyone's satisfaction only by an independent inquiry. It is most unfortunate that the Labour government has so far refused to start such an inquiry. The occasional seminar, such as that organised by the Govern-

[1] The most thorough work in this field has been done by the National Foundation for Educational Research, particularly in their two reports *Comprehensive Education in Action* (1970) and *A Critical Appraisal of Comprehensive Education* (1972). Reliable studies of GCE and CSE results in comprehensive schools in the Manchester area have also been made by Albert Spedding and R. W. Baldwin.

ment at York is a welcome sign of a change of heart, but it is not enough.

There are undoubtedly some very good comprehensive schools, achieving everything that parents want for their children. There are also some very poor ones. It is to these, and the mediocre schools, that I wish to pay attention.

Unlike the Labour Party, we believe that success should be allowed to succeed. Where schools are succeeding and carrying out their task to everyone's satisfaction, we do not wish to interfere. We only want to find from them the secret of their success.

Our aim should be to see a maintained system of education with intellectual and moral standards so high that parents will have enough confidence in it to feel that they do not have to scrimp and save to buy a private education for their children. This aim will never be achieved by the socialist nostrum of outlawing private education, which constitutes not only an act of educational vandalism but a gross invasion of human rights. On the other hand, those who are paying through national and local taxes for the educational system are entitled to the same satisfaction as those who purchase education privately. To fulfil that demand is a major Conservative aim in education.

3. Variety of schools

THE EXISTENCE of a variety of schemes within the comprehensive system is to be welcomed. It would be foolhardy to attempt to impose one system when there is so little reliable information as to which works best in practice.

Some authorities have adopted an all-through 11 to 18 system. Some have a break at 16, and provide junior or sixth form colleges for advanced work. Others have involved their primary schools in reorganisation, providing a first-middle-senior school system, with breaks at 8 or 9 and 12 or 13, and others operate mixtures of these schemes. We believe local authorities should be able to develop their schools as they see fit.

However, because severe pressures were imposed by the Labour government in enforcing comprehensive reorganisation, some hastily improvised schemes may need to be looked at again by local authorities. Many have been dictated more by questions of availability of buildings than by educational considerations. This is to some extent inevitable, but proper consideration by authorities of the alternatives has been restricted, owing to the demands of central government for speed. If these pressures are removed, many of the worst problems of comprehensives can be dealt with.

Size and type of schools

There is growing recognition of the dehumanising effect of creating huge super-schools. Some headmasters find it difficult even to know all the staff, and have little contact with their pupils. Conservatives believe that authorities should be encouraged to reduce the size of over-large schools by, for example, reversing the amalgamation of a boys' and girls' school, or extending the house system. Many schools have borrowed this from the private sector by dividing a school into two or more units. Where large split-site comprehensives have been established by combining schools on different locations, they can be separated again. These ridiculous amalgamations have rarely worked.

Of course, in some cases a large school may be working well, due to an exceptional head, and such a school should not be interfered with.

The sixth form college system has recently attracted support from the Minister of State and his officials at the Department of Education and Science. It is thought to be economical in its use of resources, providing for a wider range of courses, and attractive to sixth formers who resent school discipline. On the other hand the system deprives schools of sixth form facilities which can be used for other children, makes schools less attractive to able teachers who enjoy teaching sixth formers, and introduces a need to transfer at the age of 16 which might actually reduce the numbers going on to sixth form study.

One possible solution is the middle school system, providing for schools with a smaller age range but more children in each range, a good idea borrowed from the independent sector. These schools have advantages in curriculum since they tend to ensure that children do not specialise too early. They also provide a ready checkpoint for assessing a child's progress through the education system, and so ensure he has not missed the basic fundamentals. I do not wish to see middle schools imposed everywhere, but they make a useful contribution and ought to be given a more distinctive recognition than the official 'middle deemed primary or secondary' tag currently attached to them.

Encouraging variety

Each comprehensive school will develop its own character, through the character of its head and governors. This enhances the choice available to parents, and attempts by authorities to enforce a rigid uniformity should be discouraged. If a parent wishes to send his child to a single-sex school, or to one which does or does not allow corporal punishment, or to one where uniform is required, that choice should be open to him. The same applies to sporting and academic expertise. A school may become known for a certain sport, have facilities for tracking satellites, or teach a foreign language other than French. It may provide exceptionally good pastoral care for difficult children, or have an above-average remedial department. The development of a rich variety in our schools benefits our education service.

Comprehensive selection

The provision of real parental choice may lead to some schools being oversubscribed, and therefore involves some degree of selection. This is not necessarily a bad thing. Selection is an inevitable part of life, whether one is selecting a boyfriend or girlfriend, a football team or an employee. There are two basic methods of selection: by geography, or by ability and aptitude.

Geographical selection results from strict zoning and the enforcement of a neighbourhood school concept, where a school draws its pupils exclusively from a particular area. This introduces numerous problems, one of the most important being that children can become trapped in a poor school which reflects the conditions of a poor neighbourhood. Some authorities try to meet these problems by bussing and 'banding', but this only creates more difficulties. It assumes that children from a certain neighbourhood are mostly of one ability range, high or low, and that it is necessary to import children from another area to have the full range, an assumption now largely discredited. In any case parental preferences rather than administrative compulsion should guide the choice of school.

Some element of geographical selection is inevitable, but a more flexible system of zoning and the development of a variety of schools selecting pupils on the basis of ability or aptitude can help to resolve some of the difficulties. **This is not a return to the eleven-plus.** It means that when a school is oversubscribed it should be able to select the pupils most likely to excel at its speciality, whether that is science, languages, swimming or woodwork. If the variety in schools for which we are arguing is allowed to develop, then schools in poor neighbourhoods can be transformed into schools which are attractive to a considerable number of parents, including those who do not live in their neighbourhood. There is no reason why they too should not have a speciality from which many parents would wish their children to benefit. If necessary a local authority should take positive action to ensure that a school meets the standards parents require when choosing a school.

There must be that same parity of esteem for which the architects of the old tri-partite system hoped, if we are to stop a system of free choice leading to some schools attracting all the most able pupils.

Flexible financial arrangements are necessary if parental choice is to become a reality. It should be possible for authorities to introduce a degree of flexibility within available resources so that a popular school is able to take in more pupils, while a less popular school could introduce generous staffing arrangements which would help it to overcome its problems. This may be difficult in areas where the population is rising, but it should be possible elsewhere.

Conservatives have a deep distrust of rigid systems and panaceas for all problems. In the field of education this attitude has been thoroughly vindicated. Variety, choice, flexibility – again and again we find ourselves coming back to these words when seeking to describe the schemes we favour. There must obviously be certain limits to this variety, but if these are drawn too narrowly it is our children who suffer.

4. Organisation within the school

IT IS TO INTERNAL ORGANISATION that we must look for immediate alleviation of the problems of the neighbourhood school and the under-achievement of the bright child from a disadvantaged background.

If the comprehensive school is to fulfil its ideal, it must provide adequately for every child: the slow learner, the average and the most able. It must take the non-reader and teach him to read, the innumerate and teach him basic arithmetic. It must take the large majority of average children, identify their talents and develop them as much as possible. It must take the able child, and push him as hard as he can go so that he can meet the standards required by the most demanding university or polytechnic.

Can all our comprehensives do that now? I doubt it. Some former grammar schools are not doing as well as they should for the slow learner. Many grammar school teachers have found it difficult to adapt to the new circumstances and, after years of teaching academically-inclined children, they have found the different talents required for the other children difficult to develop.

In the former secondary modern schools some teachers have found it difficult to adapt to the new demands made by the able. In the case of neighbourhood schools in disadvantaged areas, teachers' expectations are often too low, so that many children do not achieve their potential.

The demands of the three groups of children are all different. Every secondary school should be capable of satisfying all three sorts of demands. Unfortunately not all schools are doing so.

Fixed quotas of children in each category should not be necessary in order to provide adequate classes for them. But the internal organisation of a school should be such that arrangements can be made for all the different kinds of children, except those with quite exceptional needs who require a special school. Schools should have clearly defined policies for the gifted, the average and the less able child.

Curriculum

To cater for all ability ranges, a school must develop separate curricula for each ability group. This is particularly important in the so-called 'longitudinal' subjects, that is subjects which involve the progressive acquisition of facts, such as maths, science and modern languages. A simple example is provided by mathematics for 15-year-olds.

Those at the bottom will still be struggling with the basic concepts of numeracy. The teacher's task will be to consolidate the pupil's ability to cope with the simplest tasks.

Then there will be a group studying for CSE exams. A third group may be studying to take 'O' level that year in order to take 'O' level additional maths at 16.

If a comprehensive school is doing its job properly, it will be providing all of that. Although the differences in curriculum may not be so obvious in subjects which are not strictly 'longitudinal', such as English, the principle is the same.

All this means that a teacher must select. He must identify the children in the different categories, even in a class of mixed ability. There are two quite separate approaches to this problem: either selection takes place to a greater or less extent between classes, or there is mixed-ability teaching.

Mixed-ability teaching

Mixed-ability teaching is considered by some the quintessence of the comprehensive ideal. Children not only go to a comprehensive school but are taught all subjects in a comprehensive class, where no one is selected, no one feels rejected and all are equal.

But many people, including teachers, have become alarmed about mixed-ability teaching. The evidence which is emerging from the DES itself can only deepen that concern. This is what HMIs said about mixed-ability teaching in modern languages, maths and natural science:

In modern languages: 'Where teaching in mixed-ability groups has been introduced, for good reasons, aims and objectives have been insufficiently differentiated, so that there is concern about what is happening to more able pupils as well as to those of average and below average ability. The result is that in many schools there is under-performance at all ages and stages.'

In maths: 'In some cases these problems have been accentuated by the decision to adopt mixed-ability teaching for mathematics, often for the ages 11–13, but sometimes with older children as well. . . . There are particular difficulties in teaching mathematics to mixed-ability groups. In such patterns of working some gifted teachers are outstanding examples to their colleagues. On the other hand the outcome is often limited modes of teaching, with excessive use of work-sheets, which may enable the weak to survive but which is not conducive to classroom discussion of quality. In such a climate expectation can be far too low for many children.'

In science: 'Mixed-ability teaching is an extra burden on many teachers, however willingly some of them, not by any means all, see it as an ideal. There is rightly concern that the highly able pupil should continue to be given the attention he needs.'[1]

It is clear that mixed-ability teaching makes very great demands on the teacher. The exceptional few are able to meet these demands and it would be wrong to interfere with them, but for the majority the task is virtually beyond them. Most

[1] *Mathematics, Science and Modern Languages in Maintained Schools in England, an appraisal of problems in some key subjects by HM Inspectorate*, DES, 1977: (modern languages: paragraph 3; mathematics: paragraphs 14 and 26; science: page 8). More favourable conclusions have been drawn by the Report on Banbury Comprehensive School but the circumstances at the school are exceptional, see: *Ability Grouping, The Banbury Enquiry*, David Newbold (NFER, November 1977).

teachers, and this is no criticism of them, are not up to the task.

I believe, therefore, that heads, governors and local authorities should be very wary of allowing mixed-ability teaching. A ban imposed from above would be wrong, but they should all make a special effort to monitor any mixed-ability classes. If it becomes evident that some children are suffering, mixed-ability teaching should be stopped.

This means that authorities should know where, if anywhere, mixed-ability teaching is being practised. They should also ensure that if the practice is introduced, only teachers who have received special training should be allowed to teach such classes.

As I said last July: 'With a good teacher and a highly motivated class, mixed-ability teaching can work wonders: combined with a mediocre teacher and a poorly motivated class, it is an obvious recipe for disaster.'[1]

Streaming, setting and banding

I believe it is only by the creation, within each comprehensive school, of separate classes providing for different abilities, that each child can fulfil its potential. That means the conscious creation of classes for the more able, to provide the extra push for bright children that might be denied by their home background and to overcome the consequences of low teacher expectation. And as a corollary it means classes for the less able, with the conscious application of appropriate teaching techniques to ensure that children learn the fundamentals. For just as there are fears that the able are neglected, too often there are complaints that the child who has fallen way behind in the junior school does not get the opportunity to catch up in the senior school.

There are several methods of selection within a school: banding, where children are divided into, say, three broad streams and, within the streams, are mixed in classes; streaming, dividing into classes strictly in accordance with ability; and

[1] Speech to Welwyn and Hatfield Conservative Association, 4th July 1977.

setting, which is streaming for individual subjects. My personal preference is for setting which has, after all, been an accepted and successful system in most independent schools for fifty years and more.

It is right that selection within the school should be as flexible as possible. There is no reason why someone who is good at maths should also be good at languages. Setting allows for this, so that each child can succeed to the limit of his ability in each field. So hardly anyone need feel a failure, because somewhere he or she will be making his own success. Indeed, a child who sees himself succeeding in one field may be spurred on to greater things in others.

Liaison between primary and secondary schools

Another area of organisation which needs attention is the degree of liaison between primary and secondary schools. Although the importance of knowing the full background of a child starting secondary school is generally accepted, less attention is paid to co-ordination of syllabuses between schools. Sometimes there is far too great a discontinuity and a child's education is set back by months. The reason is historical: schools have evolved with such a high degree of independence that there has in the past not been enough encouragement for co-operation. The common ground formerly provided by the eleven-plus has now been eroded. A secondary school usually has a number of feeder schools, but where there is inadequate liaison, an authority should do something about it. Teachers in the comprehensive school should be encouraged to visit classes in the feeder primary schools, and there should be more cross-fertilisation between governors and managers.

School-leaving age

In the past couple of years secondary schools have had to cope with the extra problem of the bored 15-year-old waiting to leave school. Schools have tried to meet this problem by designing courses more relevant to the needs of the non-academic teenager. Some have succeeded, some have not.

I believe that many schools could make a more concerted effort to link this last year at school with the world of work. Sound careers guidance, which should have started as early as 13, should form an important part of the curriculum by the age of 15, involving visits to local firms and the local further education college, with some short spells of work experience. In addition, 'linked courses' with the local further education college should be encouraged, since they are popular with pupils who see greater vocational relevance in the courses and appreciate the adult atmosphere of the college.

While full-time education or training in some form should certainly continue until the age of 16, it is not clear that full-time attendance at school is the best solution for all pupils. A part-time apprenticeship, with some time still spent at school or college, could be of more value to some. In all cases, early release from school should not be before the fifteenth birthday, should be with the parents' approval, and conditional on finding an appropriate apprenticeship, attending a further education college, or continuing education in the armed services.

It also makes sense for young people to continue to have access to school or college to improve their basic skills even after they have started work. Employers should not only allow their young employees to continue their studies but should encourage them to do so by day-release and block-release schemes. Their incentive to study is bound to be greater when they see how skills can be applied to their everyday work.

5. Curriculum and examinations

AT THE CENTRE of the success or failure of our schools is the question of what the children are taught. Schools are in theory free to decide that for themselves, with the exceptions of religious and physical education, and governors or managers are supposed to be involved in that decision.

The major influence, however, is not the head teacher, nor the governors. It is certainly not the parents. It is exams, the boards that set them and the Schools Council which oversees the system. These bodies provide the targets for pupils and teachers, they set standards and define curricula. They are far too remote from parents, and it is my hope that in the future we shall see the interests of parents and the community in general represented more strongly.

Decisions on the curriculum have also been influenced by the demands of further and higher education, which have indeed always dictated some kind of core curriculum. The examiners say what the content for each subject should be, the colleges say what the subjects should be. For example, only a few years ago Latin was part of any aspiring graduate's core of learning.

The introduction of the CSE helped define a curriculum for the less able who do not take GCE. But with the introduction of CSE came two new trends. First, the exam boards themselves started widening the variety of subjects available. This was a response to demands from teachers, and in its turn encouraged schools to widen their curriculum and, in some cases, distracted attention from fostering basic skills.

Secondly, the CSE boards developed new 'modes' of examining, including Mode Three. This enabled the teacher to set his own exam, in a subject of his choosing, albeit with external supervision. This encouraged even greater diversification in schools, and provided an opportunity for teachers to provide courses more suited to the less able. But it also raised doubts in some people's minds about the whole value of CSE.

There is little point in any child taking an exam just for the sake of acquiring a piece of paper. It must *mean* something; and, to be worthwhile, it must mean something to people outside the school. It follows that the exam must be a real test. And employers and parents must have confidence in the exams. After all, they are the 'customers' of the education service. They need assurance on two points, about which doubts have arisen: the validity of CSE Mode Three exams, and that standards in GCE exams have been maintained. The policy that passes a fixed percentage of exam entrants regardless of quality is wrong, and if it has been the approach in the past it should now cease to be so.

Schools Council proposals

The Schools Council now has three proposals for major exam reforms. Unfortunately, none of the proposals goes any way towards meeting the current concern for standards, a good example of how the Council is in danger of losing touch with the community.

In the same way that some people see mixed-ability classes as the ultimate in comprehensive education, so they demand a 'comprehensive exam'. They object to one exam for the less able. One exam for all, preferably with no failure, is their ideal.

The Schools Council has brought forward its proposals for a common exam at 16-plus. They are not convincing. They have failed to overcome the problem of testing the able child as well as the least able. Such are the vested interests in exams that the Council has even been unable to produce a viable administrative structure.

The imposition of this exam would encourage a common curriculum for all abilities, which in itself is undesirable. It is argued that a common curriculum would make the task of the teacher easier. The implication is that it would no longer be necessary to treat children differently. In my view the egalitarian philosophy that so opposes success, which underlies the concept of the exam, would cause lasting harm. This proposal, in which employers also have no confidence, should not go forward.

There are also proposals for a new exam at 17-plus, the *Certificate of Extended Education*. This would be for pupils who decide to stay on an extra year but do not wish to take 'A' levels, the so-called 'new sixth'. The case for this exam has not been proved. Sixth-formers who are not studying for 'A' levels can already re-sit GCE and CSE exams, study for further subjects to CSE or 'O' level or take a number of courses with a more vocational slant such as 'City and Guilds' foundation courses. There are already plenty of exams in schools; a new academic one at 17 would merely serve to confuse pupils, teachers and employers.

The idea of replacing 'A' levels with a new two-tier exam ('N' and 'F' levels) is also under discussion. It is suggested that the number of subjects usually studied in the sixth form should be increased from three to five with two or three taken at a more advanced level, slightly below that of the present 'A' level. This proposal would certainly meet the criticism of over-specialisation, but there is a real danger that it would lead to a lowering of standards. The implications of such a step need to be very carefully considered before any decision is taken, and we would like to see parents and employers fully involved in the discussions.

Basic skills

First we must identify those basic areas of knowledge in which even the least able should achieve some degree of competence. The obvious subjects are reading, writing and arithmetic, with moral or religious education. An elementary course in the arts should also form part of any school's curriculum, and one foreign language might also be included.

Monitoring standards in the basic skills of literacy and numeracy are currently the subject of much discussion. What-ever the disadvantages of the 11-plus exam, it did provide some kind of goal towards which primary school teachers and pupils could work and gave some indication of the attainment of individual pupils in basic skills. It may now be necessary to test these standards in a different way.

The target standards would not be those of CSE or GCE exams. They would be much lower. For example a reading age of 13 is considered adequate for most needs in society.[1] These standards could be tested in a number of ways that are now under consideration by our research group. One of these would be a series of tests leading to the Basic School Certificate – basic, because it would be the basic skills that were being tested.

Bright children might take these tests in junior schools or, at the latest, in middle schools. They would provide a target for less able pupils and their teachers in secondary schools.

Core curriculum

One of the difficulties facing secondary schools is that, with the ever-increasing expansion of human knowledge, they are being asked to impart more and more to their pupils in the same period of time. This has led to controversy over the degree of specialisation that should be allowed. There is also some argument over how much specific preparation for jobs should take place in schools. I think we should remember that it is not the role of schools to provide vocational training – they should provide training in general skills and their application.

Although a child at 16 may take anything up to ten subjects at CSE or GCE level, an element of specialisation will already have taken place. Some choice is inevitable, for it would be a quite impossible task to cover all the available subjects. Yet it is possible to identify major areas of knowledge – English, maths, science, modern languages, religious education and the arts – which no child should drop before the age of 16, even though he will already be favouring one or another. At present, a child

[1] According to D. Moyle, *et al: Readability of newspapers*, Edge Hill College of Education, 1973. There is some discussion about the age considered generally adequate – anything from 9 to 15 has been mentioned. There is a brief explanation of this in *A Language for Life*, HMSO, pp 10, 11 (The Bullock Report).

can drop one or more of these areas completely. And that is wrong.

One way of protecting this 'core' would be to ensure that those who do take CSE and GCE exams, the vast majority of school children, are required to take at least one exam in each major study area. Many schools do this already, and teachers in others are already convinced that this is right. It would take little administrative encouragement to ensure that it happens.

This simple move would spell the end of premature over-specialisation and ensure a balanced curriculum in every comprehensive school.

6. Parents and teachers

Traditionally the British school has evolved as an independent institution, with the head in a similar situation to that of a ship's captain. Managers and governors have a vague responsibility ('oversight') for the curriculum, which in practice is rarely exercised. Local authorities are responsible for running an efficient schools system, but in general there is a great reluctance to intervene. Many inspectors are now called 'advisers', reflecting the current philosophy on their role.

Decisions on curriculum in the different subjects are dictated by the Schools Council and exam boards in most cases, apart from Mode Three CSE. Teachers and academics control these bodies. Parents, who naturally have a strong interest in what happens in schools, have had in the past little opportunity to influence decisions. Their interest is expected to be confined to the occasional interview with class teacher and head, ensuring their children are well turned out and do their homework, and raising funds for the school. Yet bringing up children and so contributing to the next generation is the most important thing most people do in their lives. An effective say in their children's education is essential to parents' self respect.

If teachers are dealing with what is most precious to parents, they should not resent a questioning interest in what the teachers are doing to, and for, their children. At the William Tyndale junior school, some of the teachers were not interested in what parents thought and wanted. They scorned the views of parents whose ideas were different from those they themselves held so tenaciously. The result was a breakdown in confidence between home and school, and the consequences for everyone were catastrophic.

Of course, in many schools throughout the country there is a very close relationship and full confidence between parents and teachers, but the William Tyndale affair showed that it is not something to be taken for granted.

Parental involvement

Parents have a right to know what is going on in the schools to which they send their children. No school should be a closed shop. The policies, the requirements, the subjects and sylla-buses, the aims of a school, the examination results – all should be available to parents. They should be clearly set out in pros-pectuses issued by each school. Parents have got to know the strengths and weaknesses of a school. They need to know what is expected of them. There is no need for gimmicks such as unenforceable school contracts.[1] If parents know the policies of each school, and can exercise real choice, they endorse a school's policies by their choice.

Schools belong to the community. But that means more than putting councillors and friends on governing bodies. Parents are, or should be, the most important element in any lay con-trol of a school. This is now becoming accepted, and the Taylor Committee's recommendation of a balanced governing body made up of representatives of parents, teachers, local govern-ment and community interests is an excellent one which I hope will be speedily implemented by law.[2] In the meantime local authorities themselves can take the initiative, and many of them have. I would like to see a substantial proportion of governors and managers elected by parents with children at the school.[3]

Yet accountability is more than bringing the influence of the community and parents to bear on school policies. It is also about what happens when something goes wrong. It is about seeing decisions through.

Leadership

Schools cannot be completely independent. There has to be a measure of co-operation between them. For example, there

[1] A somewhat dotty idea put forward in 1977 by Mrs Williams

[2] *A New Partnership for our Schools*, HMSO, ISBN 0 11 270457 3.

[3] The idea of parent governors was one of six proposals in my speech at Stockport in August 1974 when I launched *The Parents' Charter* on behalf of the Conservative Party. The ideas set out in the *Charter* have now become generally accepted.

should be agreement on a number of points between a secondary school and its feeder schools. But when there are strong disagreements, who is to intervene? How does one maintain the advantages of independence of schools but still have a coherent system? The answer must be strong leadership from the local authority.

Leadership must not be confined to the authority and its senior officials and inspectors. Teaching has a clear hierarchy and an obvious structure. But curiously the element of leadership by senior teachers is lacking. Teachers can become very isolated in their classrooms. There is no one there to tell them what is right or what is wrong. Heads can be isolated in their schools. In many authorities a conscious effort has been made to remove the supervisory role of inspectors by renaming them 'advisers'. This situation has evolved to such an extent that the probationary teacher starting his career in school is sometimes left completely on his own, with little or no help from experienced colleagues.

This was recognised recently by HMIs, who said in their report on modern language teaching:

> 'The ideal head of department would have formulated, in consultation with colleagues, a programme of work which spelled out realistic objectives and indicated how these might be achieved. . . . He would give his colleagues day-to-day help in implementing the scheme of work, seeing them teach and being seen by them, where this would help. He would encourage their attendance at in-service courses . . .
>
> 'Almost every feature of the above portrait implies support for the junior teacher. It is sad to have to record that in something like 60 per cent of the survey schools such support was lacking to a significant extent . . .'[1]

Such a state of affairs does not help maintain standards. It means that a poor or lazy teacher can continue his inadequate teaching. No one will interfere, but the children will suffer. It is not a question of sackings or even reprimands. Long before these stages are reached the poor teacher should have access to good advice and experience.

1 *Modern Languages in Comprehensive Schools*, HMSO, 1977, pp 18-19.

Only the profession itself can put this right. Senior teachers, head teachers, local authority advisers or inspectors must accept they have a supervisory role. It should be built in to their own advanced training. It should be borne in mind when assessing the qualities of candidates for promotion. Will they be able to guide effectively those less experienced than themselves?

Employment of teachers

It is often said that it is impossible to sack a teacher, except for gross misconduct. This is not true. It is simply that it is not often done. There are proper procedures to be carried out. For example, warnings have to be officially issued. Industrial tribunals will not reverse a dismissal if it has been carried out with the utmost fairness.

Local authority inspectors are key people. They are expected to be founts of good advice, guiding teachers and head teachers. They should be able to assess new methods and advise on their suitability. Unfortunately this has not been done very well in the past. They have to be aware of how their schools are operating and must be prepared to intervene if and where necessary. To do all this demands the highest of professional skills, and in the past this has not been fully appreciated. It also demands an intimate knowledge of the class-room, and inspectors would benefit from regular spells back in school.

In the schools the most important man is the head teacher. All the recent reports of HMIs have underlined this. On my visits to schools I have found time and again that a school is as good (or as bad) as its head. Teachers have been aware of it for years too. But still too many bad heads are appointed. Why? Is it because our methods of appointment are not good enough? Certainly appointments are made in an amateur – and sometimes blatantly political – way which would be scorned by any multi-million pound industry, which is what education is. Appointment procedures should be thoroughly overhauled throughout the country under the supervision of the Secretary of State.

Education is a dynamic profession. For a head to stay in his post for twenty years or more is not necessarily a good thing. If he is a quite exceptional head, the authority may wish to move him to a school that needs some extra help. If he is not such a successful head, it may be better for him as well as the children if he is moved to a more suitable post.

The proposal that appointments should be for a fixed term, say seven or ten years, needs to be dispassionately considered. There are arguments both ways. Tenure for head teachers, like the parson's freehold, ensures independence, but the price of independence is that the system has to carry some heads who are not fit for their posts. On the other hand, a move (or even a return to the ranks) may be in the best interests not only of pupils, but of head teachers themselves.

7. Teacher training

WHATEVER ELSE one does to improve our schools, they can only be as good as the teachers who staff them. The problems all teachers, good or bad, have to face now are more complex than ever with the changes in society to which we are becoming accustomed. The demands made on them by their pupils, parents and society have never been heavier.

Teachers are entitled to ask to be backed up by their authorities so far as possible, bearing in mind the economic constraints to which local education authorities are subject. How does a good teacher acquire his talents? In one sense all you need to be a good teacher is to possess a teaching nature. Yet for everyone there must be slog – hard work, a blend of experience in the classroom and good training which enables teachers to analyse what they are doing and to improve upon it. Where authorities can help is in the training.

The Conservative Party has always been aware of the importance of training. That is why we set up the James Committee to investigate training. Unfortunately its conclusions, while receiving widespread acceptance, have never been properly implemented. They have been among the many casualties of the economic crisis.

But we cannot afford to neglect training, either at the beginning of a teacher's career or later on. I do not believe reforms need cost a lot of money. With good intentions and the right ideas much could be achieved at minimal cost.

The need for improvements in initial training was never more dramatically demonstrated than in the *Panorama* programme on the Faraday school.[1] Most teachers would agree that despite periods of classroom experience during their three years training they were ill-prepared for the real thing. Lucky teachers received guidance and help from experienced teachers.

[1] BBC *Panorama:* 21st March 1977.

Unlucky teachers were thrown in at the deep end with no assistance. The situation is the same today. There is no one to correct mistakes, as we have already pointed out, and bad habits are easily acquired.

Certainly one problem is the remoteness from the classroom of lecturers in colleges of education. However much effort lecturers take to keep in touch, unless it is possible for them to get into schools to teach they are bound to have an inadequate appreciation of the difficulties faced by teachers. I welcome any move to bring colleges of education closer to schools, by exchanges of lecturers with successful teachers, by limiting lecturers' time in colleges, or by arranging for lecturers to attend seminars held by teachers. These need cost little or nothing.

Teachers have been pressing for an all-graduate profession, and this has been accepted as an aim both by the Government and Opposition. In the future all teachers can expect to have a four-year training course leading to a degree. But this is not going to help the problems of the probationary year. With limited resources available it is far more important for the induction year to be developed as a bridge between the theory and the practice of teaching.

In-service training

The development of a well-organised and compulsory system of in-service training is more urgent than the general introduction of a fourth year in college. Introducing an all-graduate profession now at the expense of in-service training would be a misuse of scarce resources.

Training during a teacher's career has three distinct aims, depending on the teacher: to help the teacher cope with changes in his task, such as the change from selective to comprehensive education; to help the teacher keep abreast with educational thinking and improve his techniques; to correct poor techniques and bad practices.

In-service training at the moment is essentially voluntary. Those with a wish to succeed or ambition for promotion apply to go on courses. Head teachers and deputies may be asked by an authority to go on courses, and few will decline. But it is quite possible for the average teacher to go through his career without ever having any in-service training. This is wrong.

It is the responsibility of the local authority to ensure that adequate courses are available for teachers facing changing conditions in their schools. One great failure in the past has been the failure to ensure that all teachers in schools that were going comprehensive received appropriate training.

But comprehensive reorganisation is not the only change for which teachers need preparation. When a head decides to ban corporal punishment, do his teachers receive instruction in methods and approaches to discipline necessary to cope with the extra difficulties? Very seldom. When William Tyndale junior school teachers changed their methods of teaching, there was no extra instruction. As it turned out they were singularly ill-prepared for the resulting problems.

If a teacher moves from a well-disciplined academically-orientated school with a predominantly middle-class clientele to an urban school in a poor area with many immigrants and severe problems, does anyone ensure that there is a course suitable to help him cope with the change – and does anyone ensure that he attends the course?

Types of training

Preparation for promotion falls into the first category – helping a teacher keep abreast with changes in his task. It is clear that a school's success depends to a very considerable extent on the head teacher and his staff. It is also clear that a number of head teachers and senior staff are unaware of their responsibilities and the skills needed to exercise them. Candidates for promotion should have access to suitable courses, and their success in these should be monitored and recorded to provide those responsible for appointments with a guide to the teacher's abilities.

The second category – in-service training – is the one most commonly provided. But one difficulty is that sometimes only the same keen teachers attend courses. There are two possible reasons: either the local authority is mounting the wrong type of courses and they are too boring, or the other teachers are not sufficiently encouraged to attend courses. Whatever the reason, brush-up courses are important, and all teachers without exception should at intervals have the opportunity of benefitting from this sort of training.

The third category – correcting poor techniques – depends on the ability of heads of department, head teachers or inspectors to discover those teachers who for one reason or another are not succeeding in the classroom. These teachers need 'remedial training' – not to be called that, needless to say! Teachers need to be advised and if necessary directed to attend appropriate courses. A teacher who is sacked for inefficiency is entitled to object if he has not had a chance to improve.

And the cost of all this? It need not be high. It need not mean large numbers of extra appointments. The people required are all available anyway – inspectors, talented head teachers and teachers, even college of education lecturers. Much of the cost of the Government's present limited expansion is for the recruitment of other teachers while some of their colleagues are away on courses. This may be necessary occasionally, but we should remember something Lord Houghton said in his report which awarded teachers – rightly – a substantial pay increase: 'We wish to stress that we believe the salary levels we recommend justify expectations of professional standards of performance in return.'[1]

Professional people are not nine-to-five workers. Many teachers know this well enough, and I appreciate the extent of their out-of-lesson activities in the evenings, at weekends and during holidays. Indeed, some teachers already attend courses in their spare time. So in-service training does not have to be in school time – in any case the occasions when teachers would go on courses would be infrequent.

Courses vary considerably. Some may be school based, some based on the local authority, others in a region. They may last a couple of evenings, a weekend, or a few days in the holidays.

[1] *The Houghton Report on the Pay of Non-University Teachers*, 1974. Cmnd. 5848 at page 73.

There needs to be careful co-ordination of all courses by local authorities.

The crucial question at the end of all this is: should one be able to require teachers to attend courses? Marking attendance on teachers' records and taking that into account in selection for promotion may be powerful encouragement, but I believe that at the end of the day some power to require in-service training is essential.

8. Comprehensives and the private sector

THERE REMAINS THE question of the future relationship between independent schools and comprehensives. Those who oppose private education adopt two lines of argument. There is the dogmatic approach which denies the right of individuals to challenge a State monopoly in education, and there is the theory – for it is no more than that – that by 'creaming off' intelligent children private education harms the maintained system.

One cannot argue with dogmatists, but simply recognise a basic difference of philosophy in the matter of freedom and individual rights. Conservatives believe that since the right to educate children belongs to the parent and not to the State, parents have an inalienable right to educate their children privately if they so wish, provided of course that the education satisfies some reasonable standard. Indeed, by supporting the Universal Declaration of Human Rights and subscribing to the European Convention on Human Rights this has become the official view of the nation.[1]

As to the argument about 'creaming', one has only to look at the statistics of the numbers of those educated in the private and public sectors to see on what an inadequate base it rests. According to the most recent statistical survey carried out by the Independent Schools Information Service there are 302,357 pupils in independent secondary schools. Of these over 43,000 were helped to some extent by local education authorities. These figures include Scotland and Ireland and compare with over four million pupils in secondary schools in England and

[1] The United Nations Universal Declaration of Human Rights guarantees to every parent the right 'to choose the kind of education that shall be given to their children' (Article 26, para 3) and the European Convention on Human Rights (Protocol, article 2) gives a similar guarantee.

Wales alone. The maintained schools would have to be in very poor shape if they could not withstand a challenge from such a limited private sector.

In any case it is absurd to assume that all the children at independent schools are from the highest ability bracket. A broad ability range is found in private schools because by no means all of the parents of the country's brightest children choose to send them to independent schools. Some parents cannot afford to do so, others do not wish to – for a variety of reasons. Unfortunately the Labour government by outlawing grammar schools and driving the direct grant schools wholly into the private sector has reduced the opportunities for parents of modest means even further.

The 'creaming' theory rests on two false premises, one theoretical, the other practical. The theoretical false premise is that in education the system is more important than the child. Thus to ensure the existence of a totally comprehensive system the rights of the individual child and parent and the benefits of variety within the educational system have to be sacrificed. The practical false premise is that under no circumstances can comprehensive and selective schools co-exist peacefully side by side. This is a question of numbers. It is obvious that if a third, for example, of the available children are going to selective schools it is not possible to have comprehensive schools as well. But it is quite different if the percentage going to the selective schools is a lower one, say three or five per cent. In fact one can go up to ten per cent and still leave the comprehensive schools with a reasonable number of above average ability children.

Some light is thrown on this problem by the Bristol experience. There were seven direct grant schools in Bristol in a city of about 426,000 population. The proportion of Bristol City children going to direct grant schools was 4·8 per cent. A research project carried out by the schools in 1975 showed that the direct grant schools did not in fact cream off the able to such an extent that the comprehensive schools could not be comprehensive in ability. Of the Bristol children with the highest IQs (over 115) only about one in five went to direct grant schools, leaving 80 per cent to the other schools, which apart from a few independent schools were maintained schools.[1]

There is one other assumption in the argument that needs to be challenged: that a school needs a considerable number of bright children. As I have mentioned before, no one suggests that a school needs a certain number of children with learning difficulties in order to cope adequately with them. The same is true of bright children. If it is a question of 'viable sixth forms', schools and local authorities must be flexible enough to provide the necessary teaching in the school, or in other schools or colleges. If it is a question of special classes in earlier forms, it should be just as possible to make special arrangements for the bright as for those who have learning difficulties.

Assisted places scheme

The Government, pursuing dogmatic preconceptions, has abolished the direct grant system, just when the need for such schools was being more clearly demonstrated than ever. Conservatives believe that pupils within a mainly comprehensive system will benefit by having a chance of access to selective schools, and accordingly we intend to introduce a new form of the old direct grant system.

This will be done on a statutory basis, so that never again will it be possible to destroy these schools by ministerial edict or circular. In addition the direct grant will be replaced by an assisted places scheme, under which all the available money will be devoted to a partial or total remission of tuition fees in accordance with a generous income scale. The scheme would be financed by central government and parents would not have to apply to local authorities to take advantage of it.

[1] Report prepared by Dr John Mackay, former headmaster of Bristol Grammar School and published privately in 1975. The report concludes: 'The Direct Grant Schools do *not* take such a lion's share of the available talent that there is no possibility of the comprehensive school having an adequate "top" in ability and attainment. When there is no top this is the inevitable consequence of a zoned system; it has almost nothing to do with the existence of selective schools, which actually moderate the difference between one comprehensive school and another.' (page 3).

The link between the maintained and private sectors would be preserved by requiring that in order to qualify for the scheme at least 25 per cent of the entrants to the school should be drawn from maintained primary schools. The former direct grant schools would be given priority in applying for inclusion in the scheme, but the aim would be to secure a geographical spread of these schools so that parents in every region would have the opportunity of competing for a place for their children should they so wish.

One of the main advantages of the assisted places scheme is its flexibility. Schools could raise their normal age of entry to adjust their intake area or academic range, and thereby satisfy the principle of co-existence with the maintained schools in the neighbourhood without affecting their standard or well-being. By diversifying the age of entry and leaving selection in the hands of the school, the new scheme would not depend on rigid selection at a set age.

A partnership

Independent day and boarding schools have different things to offer the maintained system. Boarding schools in particular can offer something that is very scarce in the maintained sector – residential places. Day schools should be able to work with maintained day schools in the same sort of co-operation that exists between the different maintained schools. A partnership should extend beyond simply offering places to children who at the moment would not go to private schools. Certain ancillary services in a local authority, a reading and language development centre, educational psychologists, the inspectorate, for example, should be available to independent schools too, providing adequate arrangements can be worked out – but then, that is what a partnership would be all about.

Parents have already decided that peaceful co-existence between the two sectors is not only possible but desirable. Recent research carried out for the Independent Schools Information Service revealed that a considerable number of parents choose at different times or for different children both maintained and private sector education, and when they make their choice the criterion is which school would most suit their children. A new partnership, then, would simply reflect what parents themselves want.

We would expect the Department of Education and Science to continue its duty of inspecting and approving private schools. Considering the extraordinary importance of education to citizens it is obviously wrong to drop this service, which is a safeguard to which parents are entitled and which is of benefit to the community.

Clearly private education is the concern of a minority in the sense that only a few make use of it, but the existence of an alternative to a publicly financed education system benefits everyone. Conservatives do not believe in giving any special privileges to private schools, but we will not countenance the law being rigged against them. Those who serve in the private sector and parents who shoulder the financial responsibility of educating their children – and so relieve the taxpayer of a burden – are deserving more of thanks than of brickbats. The constructive way forward is not the banning of private education but the promotion of co-operation between the two sectors to the benefit of both.

9. Conclusions and summary

THIS STUDY is about the improvement of comprehensive schools. That is because Conservatives want schools, comprehensive or selective, to work well. We want parents to have as much confidence in the maintained system as they do in the private sector. The only interference we want to see in good comprehensive schools is an inquiry to find the secret of their success.

The problems

☐ The unnecessary haste in carrying out secondary reorganisation forced on local authorities by the Labour government has caused many of the problems of comprehensives.

☐ Hastily improvised schemes and inadequate facilities have now become associated, wrongly, with the comprehensive idea.

☐ Over-reliance on unproven teaching methods and unstructured class organisation has led to under-achievement among pupils.

☐ There has been a serious decline in moral and religious education which should be reversed.

☐ There should in the long term be an independent inquiry into standards of education in comprehensives.

Variety of schools

☐ Authorities should reduce the size of the huge super-comprehensives, and end split sites.

☐ The case has not yet been made out for widespread establishment of sixth form colleges.

☐ The distinctive role of middle schools should be recognised.

☐ Variety in the character and the academic, sporting and other specialities of comprehensives enhances the choice available to parents.

☐ There should be a more flexible zoning system within which oversubscribed comprehensives could select for their speciality.

☐ Every effort should be made to ensure parity of esteem between comprehensives in different areas.

☐ Schools should have more flexibility in the use of their financial resources.

Organisation within the school

☐ Comprehensives must cater equally for the slow learner, the average child and the most able.

☐ There should be different curricula for different ability groups.

☐ Mixed-ability teaching should only be carried out by teachers who have had the requisite training.

☐ Setting provides the most flexible form of internal selection.

☐ Authorities should ensure adequate liaison between primary and secondary schools.

☐ The last compulsory year at school should be more closely linked to the world of work and while the school-leaving age should remain at 16 there is room for some flexibility in practice.

Curriculum and examinations

☐ Examinations should take account of the needs and views of 'the customers' of the education service.

☐ The Schools Council proposal for a common exam at 16-plus should not go forward.

☐ A new Certificate of Extended Education at 17-plus would be likely to create confusion.

☐ Proposals to replace 'A' levels with 'N' and 'F' levels require further discussion.

☐ National standards in reading, writing, and arithmetic should be established.

☐ Early subject specialisation should be discouraged.

Parents and teachers

☐ Schools should publish prospectuses to provide information for parents.

☐ A substantial proportion of governors and managers should be elected by parents.

☐ Local authorities and senior teachers should provide more leadership to maintain teaching standards.

☐ Appointment procedures in schools should be thoroughly overhauled.

Teacher training

☐ The development of adequate in-service training should take priority over the establishment of an all-graduate profession.

☐ Teachers should receive training to help them keep abreast of changes in their tasks.

☐ Poor teaching techniques should be corrected.

☐ There should be a reserve power to require certain teachers to attend in-service training.

Comprehensives and the private sector

☐ Parents have an inalienable right to educate their children privately if they so wish.

☐ The small size of the independent sector compared to the maintained sector means that they can co-exist without major difficulty and co-operation between them should be encouraged.

☐ An assisted places scheme should be introduced to re-establish a link between the maintained and private sectors.

The author

NORMAN ST JOHN-STEVAS is Chief Opposition Spokesman on Education, an appointment he took up in June 1974.

He was educated at Radcliffe College, Cambridge, Oxford and London Universities. Called to the bar in 1953, he was first a lecturer at King's College, London, tutor at Christchurch, Oxford and then at Merton, Oxford. In 1959 he became political and legal correspondent of *The Economist*.

Mr St John-Stevas has been Member of Parliament for Chelmsford since 1964. He has published many books, and is a well-known broadcaster on both radio and television.

From June 1970 to November 1972, he was Secretary of the Conservative Party Home Affairs Committee. In November 1972 he was appointed Parliamentary Under Secretary of State at the Department of Education and Science. In December 1973 he became Minister of State for the Department until the election in February 1974.

In March 1974 he was appointed Vice-Chairman of the Conservative Education Committee, and in May 1974 Opposition Spokesman on the Arts, a post he retained on being appointed Opposition Spokesman on Education.

OTHER CPC PUBLICATIONS ON EDUCATION

How to save your schools
A survey of the basic rights of parents,
governors and teachers and the powers of
the Minister of Education, by Norman St John-
Stevas MP and Leon Brittan MP
CPC No 573, July 1975   50p

Parental choice
A pamphlet by Dr Rhodes Boyson MP on the
need for participation and freedom in
education.
CPC No 561, January 1975   15p

Raising educational standards
A CPC discussion brief issued in the Three-
Way Contact series.
CPC No 590c, August 1976   5p

The lessons of Tyndale
An examination of the William Tyndale affair,
by Paul Williams, a former editor of *The Teacher*
CPC No 599, March 1977   40p

CONSERVATIVE POLITICAL CENTRE
32 Smith Square, Westminster,
London SW1P 3HH. Tel: 01-222 9000.

THE CONSERVATIVE POLITICAL CENTRE

through its books and pamphlets sets out to stimulate thought and discussion of new ideas within the Party and outside. It also provides background and briefing material on a wide variety of political topics.

For a subscription of £3·75 per annum you can receive a copy of all new CPC pamphlets on publication at a substantial saving in cost. Further information from the address below.

CPC literature subscribers also receive an invitation to CPC national functions.

CONSERVATIVE POLITICAL CENTRE
32 Smith Square, Westminster,
London SW1P 3HH. Tel: 01-222 9000